PERCEPTIONS OF REALITY

Edited by

Heather Killingray

First published in Great Britain in 2002 by
POETRY NOW
Remus House,
Coltsfoot Drive,
Peterborough, PE2 9JX
Telephone (01733) 898101
Fax (01733) 313524

HB ISBN 0 75434 337 5
SB ISBN 0 75434 338 3

FOREWORD

Although we are a nation of poets we are accused of not reading poetry, or buying poetry books. After many years of listening to the incessant gripes of poetry publishers, I can only assume that the books they publish, in general, are books that most people do not want to read.

Poetry should not be obscure, introverted, and as cryptic as a crossword puzzle: it is the poet's duty to reach out and embrace the world.

The world owes the poet nothing and we should not be expected to dig and delve into a rambling discourse searching for some inner meaning.

The reason we write poetry (and almost all of us do) is because we want to communicate: an ideal; an idea; or a specific feeling. Poetry is as essential in communication, as a letter; a radio; a telephone, and the main criterion for selecting the poems in this anthology is very simple: they communicate.

CONTENTS

UNTITLED

Curled in this shell of most fragile love
That cracks with fear and grows
With each day's learning
Your eyes unblinking
Stare me into safety
Cast me softly into
Hay-smelling summers
Lull me in fireside snug

I am a wild creature
Yet so frail also
Fearless in the face of injustice
Terrorised by a loud noise
Or words spoken in anger

This strange life ahead
Coils far into the distance
Frees and suffocates
Your eyes unblinking
Wrap me round in silence
Turn me towards the sun

The great world turns
I am, as a drop of rain
Privileged to fall.
Love freely given
Stays in this world
The heart is never
Too full for more

Your eyes unblinking
Are sacred
For they carry it.

Helen Garrett

THE SIESTA SILENCE

boot treads on gravel path
he seeks surprise
of his arrival
head turns - eyes follow

dumbing of siesta sun
insects' thighs strain in
breathless consummation

two bodies entwine
unravel - spent
aware of quiet

a listened silence
boots on gravel
the lock unlocked

the door heel-booted
in alarm flesh
by fear bruised

two shots ring out
twin silenced
in prayer united

he wipes his hands
sweat on dampness
sounds of boots
on arid gravel

Michael Fenton

ESCAPE

I sit atop a mountain and stare at the land below
all around is green and cool and feeds my weary soul.
Far from the city's violence I have fled
with daily stories of who is dead.

So here for a brief hour,
I share a tranquil scene
knowing much to my sorrow that
this is but a dream.

The real world is that of death
and senseless brutal killings,
spawned by greed for power and
a wanton disregard for life.

So when, oh when,
my tired, tortured soul asks
will you have had enough?
How many more must go before your guns
before the killing beast is sated.

P L Brassington

SMALL

I live in a small world
Which is very full and fairly tidy.
Most things slot neatly into their places.

I find I am able to be
Many things to many people.

New bodies and new lips
Brush past my life
Filling much the same positions,
Leaving much the same impressions.

Change goes on around me:
I know there are things wrong outside;
But there's only one of me;
What can I do about them?

There are things I mean to do
But don't get around to.
I've only so much time;
And so many things I just can't put off.

People have their parts to play;
People have their parts;
But sometimes I'm not sure about mine;
And then, I find myself:

Trying to be in all the places,
Competing with some unknown faces
And sometimes it seems
There are just too many possibilities.

So . . . I live in a small world
Which is very full and fairly tidy.
I live in a small world
Which is very full and fairly tidy.

Gayna Florence Perry

UNTITLED

Evening comes early on these days
And I can't walk so good
I'm saying things I didn't think
Tripping over again

I love the mindless vandalism
Give the little kiddies guns
Heart-shaped rocks
So tenderly flung

Ben Cassidy

FATHERS AND DAUGHTERS

'You're grounded my girl.'
(Enters room, slams the door.)

'Thanks a lot, Dad.'
(Drags her feet across the floor.)

'Save the sarcasm.'
(Places hands on his hip)

'I wasn't sarcastic.'
(She bites bottom lip.)

'Enough of the attitude.'
(He waves arms around.)

'What bloody attitude!'
(She gazes at ground.)

'No need to swear.'
(Shaking his head)

'I didn't swear.'
(Scratching her leg)

'Oh don't start.'
(He frowns, he sighs.)

'I'm not!'
(She rolls her eyes.)

'Just go to your room.'
(He points at the door.)

'I'm going, I'm going . . .'
(Exits room - slams door.)

(He tuts)
(She stamps upstairs)

(He curses)

(She doesn't care.)

Upstairs - leaving for good.
Downstairs - wishes he could.

Cathrine Wignall

THE SILENT CRY

In silence, she cried; but pleaded for mercy not!
Regal in her silver bark, elegant and tall, in that
bright spring; deceptive, morning light.
A morning, of birdsong and pregnant with hope.

Seemingly, like, so many mornings she had seen before, in
her young and vibrant life and yet not; as this was a
morning marked for despair, betrayal and death.
Graceful was she in life so her felling, her delimbing
brought with it a hideousness, an ugliness, an unfitting end.

Though trembling before the cold, cruel teeth of the
Woodmen's saw her fall was unchecked, her death
unheard; save for a groan, and cracking of limbs. More
dreadful, still, was the poison's task to deaden the call of
next year's spring.

Spring's, loud, insistent call would undoubtedly beckon
forth the new; the innocent fragile buds of life.
And yet for all springs promise this birch would fail to hear
its call; for her the promise rang hollow, vain and futile,
as she lay mutilated, and grotesquely felled.

Silently, compassionately, she cried for the Crow, the Dove
and the visiting Hawk; as their homes, entwined with her
life, were abruptly destroyed. Tears, also, she shed for man's
hardness of heart, as uncaring, unaware of her purpose in life.

Simply a tree! What value her life, as her cry went unheard,
and her death unmarked; uncaring, unthinking his use of the
tree; as nature he used for his ends alone! Unfeeling is man of
the beautiful birch so he sweeps from his view its elegant shape.

Felicity M Greenfields

CHILD IN YOU

Golden locks and eyes of blue
The child gone in me, is now in you.
Sweet smiles about your face enthral me
Lifts my spirits, when I feel low.
Tiny hands and a gentle whisper
A cherubic face makes me glow.

Short are days, you'll stay this way
But in my picture's mind
Is imprinted beauty child
Of the sweetest gentlest kind.

Vivien Jane Bailey

X + Y

X
X is forgotten by so many,
Remembered by so few.
They are odd.
Odd if they do obey it,
Unodd if they do not.
Remembered by Jesus,
Forgotten by more . . .

Y
You either aren't,
Or you are.
Born with it,
Nothing you can do about it.
It's like a tag around your neck,
Only it says more than just 'I'm stupid.'
People have been killed because of it.

XY
Put them together,
You have the ultimate 'freak',
Only they are not the 'freaks'.
'Chocolate biscuits in domes!'
Some may call.
See what I mean.
See what I mean.

D C Wright

DO I HAVE FREEDOM?

Do I have freedom beyond the skin?
Where my feelings are buried within
The very heart people do harm
When they kick my leg or punch my arm.

Do I have freedom, for I am trapped?
There are invisible chains my
Wrists have clapped.
My ankles are bleeding.
I'm locked to the wall.
Nobody hears when I shout or call.

Do I have freedom, I am alone?
With only my skin, to warm my bone
No love, no warmth, no friends by my side
They have all left me, to run and hide.

Do I have freedom to make my own choice?
Can I have a chance to hear my own voice?
Can I just breathe and sigh alone
Or can I have company to warm my bone?

Do I have freedom, to be happy and laugh?
No, I don't
I am no whole, but I am half.

Danielle Trebert

IT'S THE WAITING

It's the waiting
for what one knows what.

It's the waiting
for dawn's ending long night.

It's the waiting
for the seasons lawn mowings end.

It's the waiting
for the end of long winter's nights.

It's the waiting
for the end of wine's dreaming need.

It's the waiting
for loving wives' 'choice' dress choice.

It's the waiting
for ones loved ones needful return.

It's the waiting
for a life success to provide all the answers.

It's the waiting for someone to care.

It's the waiting
For mother's baby's birth release.

It's the waiting. It's the waiting. It's the waiting
For the feeling that all's been worthwhile.

K Chesney-Woods

WHY?

He's dying
And there's nothing they can do
But watch helplessly,
As each hard won breath
Causes the tiny fingers to clench,
And deepens the pain-etched furrows
That mar his tiny face.

He drew his first breath
On the ward upstairs
Barely a month ago.
Now, thanks to a stray bullet
Meant for his mother's dealer,
He'll end his life down here,
Surrounded by plastic and tubes.
Sometimes, even the hardest hearts
Are forced to weep.

Clare Anne Lewis

QUIETUDE!

It is the quiet that I crave, the blessed soothing calm!
Not yet the quiet of the grave, nor Lethes drowsing balm.
I dream of where the heather blows - on some high purple-moor,
There on the breeze is heard the Curlews cry,
Far from the clamouring urban roar where
widening vistas meet the arching sky!

Or to a dell where morning dew bends low the fragrant Thyme,
A babbling brook beneath the Willows shade,
The fragrant air so sweet and cool, as sparkling Champagne wine
and Turtle-doves coo softly in the glade.

Not only in some sylvan-glade does quietness reside,
It lingers when the evening shadows fall,
My love and I, contented sit around the fireside
and pensively the long lost days recall.

And then content, with quiet mind, my reverie fulfilled, the hearing
cleansed, the vision cleared, the moral now instilled.
I'll seek the quiet paths to tread, let calmness be my guide,
leave Vulcan to his nosy trade, whilst I serene abide!

Leonard Muscroft

MATTINS

Birds break first light's mute expectancy
With vernal call-signs that announce: 'The Sun is up!'
And excitement, that once more it's peeked
Like a father performing a trick to his child
Who demands, 'Do it again . . . do it again.'

Songthrush, mistlethrush, blackbird,
Open their philharmonic throats
To orchestrate an orgy of decibels
That pre-empt the milkman's tintinnabulation
And commuter-car cacophony:

Welcoming fresh life
And awakening light sleepers
(Who turn like doors on creaky hinges)
To an improbable crescendo of silence

Broken by a close insistent cock-crow.

David Sewell Hawkins

LIFE'S CANVAS

Life is one big canvas we paint a little every day
Our picture takes on greater depth as we pass along the way
As for all the colours although we may not choose them
The beauty of our picture depends on how we use them

We must not paint our picture as though we're in a rush
We need to contemplate and stop to clean our brush
Sometimes we will be painting as though we are inspired
Another time our brush seems stiff, making us feel tired

Our picture requires much effort and inspiration too
Thought, care and attention in everything we do
Our picture is not destined for some exhibition hall
It is to be presented to the greatest judge of all.

Mary Shepherd

APPLES OF GOLD

His mouth is most sweet
And everyone wondered,
At teachings so gracious
Unheard of before
Refreshing, endearing,
And everyone followed
And thirsty listened
By Galilee's shore.
They wanted to hear Him
The crowds sad and weary
With need to be hear Him
The rich and the poor
And adults and children
They jostled and mobbed Him
And multitudes clung
On words, fitly spoken
That fell from his tongue
Heart-touching ideas
And stories He told,
Like pictures, in silver
Of apples of gold.

Christina Hanson

I LIKE ME

I am not ashamed I like me
The badness in me
Is what other people see
But I am afraid you are wrong
Because you see
If you look at yourself
You're just a reflection of me

I am made of bones
And I have also overtones
I have flesh that is weak
Is that what you seek?

Because I am different
Does that make me a freak
Hey there man what is it you seek?
Because I have not you brag
Because I am different
I am a fag hey Mr Wonderful

What would you be?
Because I am different
It's what makes me
Now Mr Perfect
That's why I like me

A E Marshall

NOBODY KNOWS

She is four years old.
She is asleep and she is dreaming.
Of what does she dream.
Alone in her bed?
Nobody knows.

She dreams of two children
Playing games in the shade.
What game do they play
In that creaking old boat?
Nobody knows.

The game is a secret.
She'll not tell a soul.
Who taught her to be silent
To be afraid and ashamed?
Nobody knows.

Nobody knows the secrets
That darken her lonely soul.
Nobody knows the fears
That chase her through the night.
Nobody knows.

Kate Chandler

SUMMER SOLSTICE

Stonehenge stands sentinel in the middle of the Plain:
testament to Man's technology.

As the eastern sky turns to gold
at Midsummer solstice,
caressing the lucky horseshoes with light,
shadows of mighty trilothons stretch
towards the bluestone altar.

And at the altar, the high priest stands,
whilst white-rob'd figures wait.
The Druids' Dawn Chorus swells
to greet the rising Sun,
enveloping this miracle of time,
as the annual celebration plays out
the mystery that is Stonehenge.

Joy Morton

TURNSTONES

On legs like lines
Drawn in pink pencil
On the harbour wall,
Turnstones tear along the quay
Feet a blur, too fast to follow,
Hoofing hotfoot

And

Stop

To pick pick pick
With a black thorn of a beak
At some minute morsel

Or stand,
Motionless mascots,
On the boat's bollards

Or

A brown and white blur
On flickering wings
Whistles across the water.

Roger Butts

BEING

Like forgotten islands we live,
Some hard, impenetrable rocks
That fight off relentless waves,
Some soft, crumbling with each new surge.
Yet our enigmatic hearts remain dry,
Uncompromised by the ferocity of these elements;
Baked by blistering sun,
Frozen in a desolate wind,
Drowned by indomitable deluge -
And only briefly do the rainbows form.
Yet this ephemeral flood of colour
May bathe our eternal causeways
And allow us a glimpse into the void within;
Like a flurry of bats hitting food in the night
Our somnambulist dream is fleeting but lucid.

Stephen J Isaac

NOTHING TO COMPARE

The cracks in the sunburnt soil
are nothing compared
to the scars
left on my heart
the day you walked away

The floods angry rivers cause
are nothing compared
to the tears
my eyes have cried
for you many a day

The explosions awoken volcanoes make
are nothing compared
to the beat of my heart
when after so long
you finally came my way

Oriana Cipriani

LEAN AGAINST THE SUN

L-Lean against the sun,
Incline your face into low-angled rays,
Slow breathe and walk a zombie walk to warmth,
Blur half-closed eyes, rotate a cross of light,
And feel your face bestowed with radiance;
Your S.A.D, each pore relieved to know
The iron-filings-to-a-magnet pull
The force of life upon your skin, your lips
Just you, inside a beam's bestow - exclude all else -
And ask: Where is my church but here?

E-ease into the poetry,
Incline your ear into an arch of sound,
And nod and love the lilt of stress, unstressed,
The wash of words, the best that man can do
And feel your mind instilled by wisdom's light,
Your E.S.P your thoughts enrapt to know,
The gentle ministry of love and grace,
The speaking of your heart through time,
Just you, an echoed ode - inspiring to aspire
And ask: Where is my church but here?

Steve Kendall

THE MOON

I wonder by the stream by day,
And by the stream by night,
And there is no one to turn to
Except,
The moon alone!

I have no friends,
I have no foe,
I have no one at all,
There is no one in the world for me,
Except,
The moon alone!

Whenever I am lonely,
The moon is all I see,
So there is no one for me,
Except,
The moon alone!

J C Una-Kell

TEMPO

The tempo of this racing organ,
Engages the emotional state,
Embracing heartfelt feeling,
In a way that cannot defy fate.

In such a flux of feeling,
All joy contained within,
That leaves the head reeling,
And lets chemistry, apparent begin.

The sparks that I feel,
Can only reveal the depths of emotion within,
Central to all of me, a palpitating real reminder,
Beating motion that sets the seal.

Susie Belt

To M C Escher
(Artist of stairs and uphill running water)

You are Dutch, I British.
That which you draw, distinctly Flemish.
With the wash-clear light of the polder
and the geometry of dykes.
Full of the unnatural forces
that push the very sea uphill.

You map with equal worth,
Three distinct and different types of north.
Logic in the eye of the beholder.
Different ground, different sky.
To take the unfamiliar views,
I am eyes open, tongue still.

Robert Paul Cathmoir

WALKING

I walked the streets, that autumnal day,
Wrapped in memories which had passed
Their sell-by date years ago.
Looking into strangers' faces,
Popping into my viewfinder, I thought
How everyone seems related somehow,
Without ever realising it.
A mother, a child herself, pushed her pram;
Older than me, than her, than all of us,
Perhaps this was the new incarnated one,
Come around once more to finish the job.
I walked on, shopkeepers were preparing
To close the day's business and -
Return to more pressing matters
And more familiar affairs,
Conducted in semi-privacy
Located in would-be English castles.

The eye sees too much,
Far too much for comfort.
While there is unease in this,
In almost everything,
I must just carry on
And make some sense.

Richard James van der Draaij

SONG OF THE DEAF

Swirling tides of angry sound
break forth around my head.
It's like the wind raging in a desert
stirring up sand and lost vegetation
until it storms through the frightened air
filling up the eyes and mouth and ears
of travelling people.
Until trembling they fall
grow quiet and die
consumed by what they live on.

It is like that for the deaf.
Not the silence you imagine
not the easy edging into tranquillity.
For us no cool rivers
cleansing hot flesh and the sweat of the day.
For us no green lavender-scented shades above
no calm and solid earth beneath.

So do not raise your voice when you find me, stamping
your desires into my sound-drowned heart.
No, rein in your busy words
trap your tongue, let your lips be still.
And watch me.
Read my face, my eyes, my hands.
Echo my thoughts
spun in the patterns my fingers make in the air.
Close your ears
enter my world
and see.

A L Brooke

THE GRAND DELUSION

With the downfall of yesterday's superficial giant of mediocrity
we raise on high today's new incumbent,

with penurious platitudes and vacuous endorsements he greets us,
and we cry out in impotent joy at the top of our voices
at the newly crowned vagabond,

inanities ring forth from his shiny mouth with a resounding echo,
poorly reflecting sincerity
and filling the empty places with an abundance of insignificance,

like mercury his words flow,
unstoppable and poisonous through our already contaminated souls,

until,

within the space of a heartbeat,

we are once more thrown back into harness to await the next lie.

Thomas Frail

THE WALK BEHIND
(Dedicated to my lovely mother, Mae, who died 24th Feb 1990)

The sky was grey and heavy, as we left that early morn,
My heart was sore and breaking,a ghost amongst the living.
The wood was warm and golden, and the brass so brightly polished,
My brain was dull and foggy, like I was only dreaming.

I did the walk behind her, my thoughts all running riot,
Her kindly face before me, a smile through all the quiet.
The crowd were mumbling softly, all my senses long since gone,
The lonely, broken soulmate, who was left to carry on.

The walk was long and sombre, as the rain began to fall,
I saw her lie before me, in her lacy, satin gown.
The car was black and glistening, no reflection in its glass,
Our final walk together through the memories of the past.

I did the walk behind her, all the way to Heaven's door,
The ground so soft and soggy, as the silence filled the air.
And as they laid her gently in her bed beneath the stars,
She squeezed my hand and whispered, 'I was with you on your walk.'

Donna McGlinchey-Mahon

ON CLIMBING THE AONACH EAGACH RIDGE BEFORE DAWN

Starlight, all that you leave behind,
Dissolves onto the grey, cracked rocks.

Alone at dawn, the mountain and I,
The dusty darkness, the cloudless sky.

Through the clear air, fading moon,
I'll stand here until it grows once more.

Tobias Monk

WIDE-OPEN SPACE

A wide-open space,
With freedom for me.
Both beautiful and pure,
Both simple and calm.

Feelings aren't scared to be shown.
Thoughts aren't scared to be ridiculed.
Belief in yourself grows
In this wide-open space.

No longer wishing to read others' minds,
No longer trying to be what you're not,
No longer wishing you were someone else.

A wide-open space
With freedom for me.
It's beautiful and pure,
It's simple and calm.
How many others want
A wide-open space?

Carrie Stuart

LARA DOESN'T LIVE HERE ANYMORE

Lara's perfect adult body was
Trapped by a child's rainbow-coloured mind.
'In love' she hungrily dived in head first,
Leaving care and caution far behind.
A free spirit, desperately searching for her soulmate.
Self defeated, she thought it was too late.
Disillusioned, she sold out, trying *too* hard to please.
Starved of love and affection she was sucked into
The Black Abyss with ease.
Don't come knocking on her door.
Lara doesn't live here anymore.
Repeatedly rejected, let down, left alone,
Her self respect left tattered and torn.
Lust for a 'good time' doesn't last
Regrets are many,
If you dwell in the past.
She had always admired and respected 'him' from afar.
He got too close. She went too far.
Broken promises, shattered dreams,
Sleepless nights and unanswered screams.
Don't come knocking on this door,
Lara doesn't live here anymore.
One frosty morning they found her
She'd taken her own life,
She had tried to once before.
Lara had traded in
Her restless soul for a risk-taking addiction.
'Gonna die before I get old'
Was her ominous prediction.
Flirting with death,
She'd painted her face for her fatal last date.

Leaving no forwarding address she checked out
Embracing her untimely fate.
Don't come knocking on this door
Lara's moved on, she doesn't live here anymore.

Amelia Michael

THE WOOD CARVER

It's just a tin shed: unprepossessed
in corrugated green and dull patches.
You would hardly know it was there.
But inside - ah yes - inside . . .
The wonderful inviting clutter;
always warm;
'a nice place to be'
as the living timber is sliced clean.

I remember - oh yes - years ago -
he first whittled a crude horse . . .
maybe still in some attic, galloping in the darkness
across some now forgotten prairie.
It only took a penknife and wanting to do it
but was not easy.
Afterwards, the rest followed quite naturally.

And now: rows of gleaming chisels and gouges -
ash handled, oiled, brass bound -
are honed to the correct angles:
each to make the work simply done.
The chips fly off in unthinking crispness.
It is the wood which tells the chisel where to cut,
and on the floor, dust and shavings:
the material that is not used.

Instinctive hands:
no longer a barrier between eye and grain.
But still he dreams longingly of exotic timbers
and their qualities.
Whilst he is working in his shed:
so I in mine; carving my words.

Peter Jones

NEVER AGAIN

Barely heard. From behind closed doors
Tongues twitter. Sharp knives clatter.
It is night. Fierce red light shifts.
Through a cluttered sky as stars
Flare beyond our sight. We're blind.

Those sensuous fingers can't be yours
But the pasts, which lingers. Let's
Listen for that broken music of the
People. It is also ours and more so
In coming momentous hours. Cherish
That harmony that once was. But now
It is almost no more. It dies. A cripple.

Persistent echoes are still heard. Minds
Harden. And across the great waste shimmers
A hot horizon. Too many never ever perceive
Or even hear the thistle rustle. Our love
May surface again. And yours too. Just whistle.

Dust clears. Dark laments rise and fill our
Ears. Yes, we hear, we hear the airs. Each
Note addresses those who would kill. Crash
Of sounds, orchestra of revenge and hate
As minds no longer wander. For we remember.
We knew, and say never again. No, never again.

Jack Withers

THE ELEPHANT MAN

Tortured by the glass reflection
Mirroring more imperfection
Abomination personified
A representation justified

Bulbous head on twisted frame
Known only by a sideshow name
A hideous freak inanimate
Exhibited to obfuscate

The product of all loveless dreams
Inciting cold and heartless screams
A blistering mass, a human mess
Deformity taken to excess

Beyond the repulsive outer shell
I let the true John Merrick dwell
He who lives with handsome face
He who moves with style and grace

Emerging from the mortal shroud
Insignificant in the hostile crowd
Congruous to those I meet
Accepted as the man complete.

J Williams

THE CHARGE

'Charge for the guns! Forward, the Light Brigade!'
(Last night I dreamed Love lured me to her bed,
With soft white arms, and silken tressèd head.)
Heed not the shot; orders must be obeyed.
Though volleys roar, trust to the naked blade!
(Upon the sheet the virgin flower blushed red.
What though before tomorrow I be dead,
Last night, my love - oh the wild charge we made!)

Hearts' hoofbeats pounding, hell for leather, leap
The redoubt; drive home each thrilling sabre-thrust,
Daring the cannon's mouth which, jarring deep,
Ejaculates its full Vulcanic lust -
A brief transfiguration, searing white -
Then, in the dark of Death, scream for the Light!

Bernard Brown

FEAR

Out of the corner of my eye I see it moving.
Out of the darkness it comes.
Slowly I run, blinded by my ignorance, stumbling forward.
Attempting to reach the distant haven.

Studying my every move.
Calculating the onslaught.
Waiting for a chance . . .

I stagger and stop.
Frozen with fear.
My every breath echoing an eternity,
My every action is life repeated,
My existence at an end.
My suffering just beginning!

Christopher McFetridge

VIA DOLOROSA

What a din, and what an uproar,
What a clangour and a clamour!
What tramping stamping of the feet,
Shouting, hounding, down the street!
In the distance, who is this
With heavy beam on stricken shoulders,
From the motley crowd appears?
Ragged, dusty, bleeding, bending,
With His sweat like tears!
Flash of sun on soldiers' helmets,
Flash on guarding spears.
Seething mob with spitting, cursing,
Mixed with sneers and jeers!
See, He passes, gasps and gazes
At the gloating evil faces,
And lifts up His swollen eyes
While the steep road treading - staggering -
Looks to yonder hill where crosses
Very soon will rise!
While like a barrage, screeching voices
Fill His ears with
'Crucify'

Kathy Breakell

ATTACK

Agitation builds momentum as icy fingers of fear
slice through anticipation signifying it's only moments to meltdown.

The heart becomes pounding fists upon the door of a vault
with skins prickling clamminess reminiscent of being buried
in wet sand.

Air is taken by force and compressed into shallow ineffectual gasps and
the mouth becomes a woollen wasteland of aridity.

Eyes witness silver-sparkled flitting fairies and everything's heard
through the buzzing whine of an echoing chamber.

Adrenalin cries, 'Fight, faint or flee!'
Then the brain makes its choice and ground gains altitude
as panic swallows its victim whole.

Susan Greenhalgh

THE HEDGER

The tools seem crude, made by the village smith,
gossock and axe and splasher, leathern mitts
(all might have served to fight on Naseby Field,
but now constrained to a more peaceful use)
they're all he needs to change a thicket mass
of blackthorn, whitethorn, holly, ash or elm
 - some to discard and some to pleach and shape
then pin with stakes to make a tidy hedge -
to hold the stock in neatly cordoned fields.

A winter job when leaves which clothed the trees
are drifted in the ditch, an eiderdown
for dormouse, hedgehog, where the pheasants scratch
in rainbow plumes and vainly strut their stuff.

He, blended with the hedge, does not disturb
the robins as they mark their bound'ries out,
the titmice troop pass by without a glance,
or blackbirds pairing off in each false spring
nor hares that box and prance in frosted grass.

The sun which rose above the sombre wood
feebly dispelled the mist along the brook
Now sinks to leave the air a sering cold.
The cow's breath smokes around the cattle ring.
The hedger bags his tools and makes his way
To lamplit table and to welcome fire.

David Griffiths

MORNINGS IN MARCH

So bright, so clean, so fresh,
Yet clear and cold.
The sun stares through a frosted pane,
The air tingles, newly exposed,
Trees still stark, warriors standing watch.
Trip back to my warrior days,
Day trip to Hastings in March.
Museums, curios, cafés, passed above us.
She was the conqueror,
And I, one-eyed Harold,
Back from the dead.
We filled whole pages of the Domesday Book.
Each passer-by took his place, listed with his possessions.
'Ah, now he definitely owns two cows,'
'And he's got a pig under his jumper.'
We turned a page and the desolate beach was upon us,
We saw the ships roll in, banners streaming,
We were armies, clashing for attention.
The conqueror would decide.
Yet Harold would not be defeated now.
The force from above separates the armies,
The conqueror cries and rages, hugs no comfort.
Harold stands aloof, gazing at a poem washing in with the tide,
Chastisement washes over her unbroken.
So bright, so clean, so fresh,
Yet clear and cold.

Paula Holt

TIME STOOD STILL

Time stood still
Amidst the fighting came a lull
A still silent calm.

Clash of combat
Cowering, cringing,
People mourning
Loved ones lost.
Time stood still.

Debris everywhere,
Panic reigned.
Mothers weeping
For the silent dead.
Time stood still.

Jets soaring up above
Where was the God of love?
Reflecting on the sins of man
Whilst time stood still.

Rosalind I Caygill

SAMSARA (HINDU - REBIRTH)

When I shall die
Think only this of me
That I will never want to see
This world or dismal century again.

It's said a soul can reappear
In someone else's flesh and blood.
Heaven forbid that I should want to be
Reincarnated as a naked pawn
In a distraught world's gruesome destiny.

If by chance one had been born
At another time, in another place,
One could be ripe for slaughter in a trench
Crawling with cockroaches and lice
And the stench of rotting comrades in the slime.

With no better luck
One might have been a Jew in Hitler's Reich
Ghettoed and harried like a sewer rat
Despatched to a frightful fate in Buchenwald.

One might return as a refugee,
As child or mother, or a starved old man,
With handcart, grimy rags and blistered feet
Fleeing a senseless war of spite, revenge,
Greed, ambition or utopian dream.

Millions have passed away
Unnoticed and unsung,
Living their lives in pain and dread,
Hard labour, poverty and sour despair.

I do not want to pass this way again.

Ray Racy

TOM THROUGH THE LOOKING GLASS

He starts very slowly to clean his paws, (thinks)
If I sit here longer there might be more.
What's that? He moves quickly, there is someone there
It's that fellow again. He didn't half stare.
As fast as I try to catch him out
He follows me around and then stares me out,
'It's puzzling'
Who is this fellow? He looks like me.
I've tried to get in there, and he's tried to get out.
He mimics my movements, each time he's about.
If I throw him a look, which says 'Well if you dare!'
He'll just sit and stare and doesn't turn a hair.
'It's puzzling'
I'd like to be friends, he looks so alone.
Sitting there with his toys; as if turned to stone.
Look, he's stretching, he's yawning, just like me.
I think I'll take my nap and wait for my tea.
Now would you believe it?
He's doing the same.
Can't anyone tell me this fellow's name.
He's never outside, I like playing in the flowers,
I've searched for him for hours and hours.
Seems he's only there when I have my tea.
Ah! Now I know, why did I not see?
It's zany, it's not puzzling, it's just silly old me.

D Rodgers

DRIVING TO WORK

I turn up the radio
to try to drown out
the noise in my head.
Some girl sings about
flying like a bird
and I want to
switch off her mouth.
On medium wave,
the world is 'alright with me'.
I flick the knob to zero
and listen to mindless chatter
about the washing-up and how
I'm late for work
again.

Erika Martin

NOT GONE BUT FORGOTTEN

No one wants a hero
Not today at any rate
If you're brave and courageous
Then you're sixty years too late

They cheered and applauded
When he carried the nation's flag
Now he carries his belongings
Inside a carrier bag

They might have understood
If he had lost a leg
It was his mind that was injured
So he has to stand and beg

Sleeping in the subway
Near a main line station
Being told to 'move along'
By a selfish ungrateful nation

It's 'Sod you, Jack'
You're getting in the way
No one wants a hero
Well, not today

Bob Gates

THE HUMAN RACE

There never seems to be enough time, it travels by so fast,
always when you're having fun, it never seems to last,
dashing here and dashing there, at a very quickened pace,
you really would think Human Beings, were in some sort of race.

Time is of the essence, I've often heard it said,
get up quick, the alarm is sounding, get out your lazy bed,
Transport's getting faster, to take you here and there,
people talking on mobile phones, you see them everywhere.

I wonder where the technology is going, or where it's going to end,
thinking about it in my head, drives me round the bend.
The computer age is here now and moving very fast,
without it now, the human race is never going to last.

Steve Elson

A COMING

Seek
climb
through opaque knowledge
masked light
from blackened sun.

'Energy is all,' said one comforter;
'Ugliness has edge,' another said;
'Depths have shallows,' bled a third.

Yet the child cried 'I fear to live.'
And the elder echoed, 'I fear to die.'

. . then the snow christened -
hushing,
smothering
a silent white beauty covering all;
the dove flew
total revealed
inevitable trust beyond human powers;
a listening eternity
dispelling fear;
bliss breaking through
as sun through cloud.

The Babe born

concordance of trust
healing the agonies of imprecision
a certainty of sacred space for all.

Then the child sang, 'I long to live!'
And the elder sang, 'I long to die!'

David Bowes

GLIMPSES OF THE PAST

Look not to the future,
If you ignore the past.
For who is to say,
That the future is not already history.

Helen Walker

THE STORM

Green blackness briefly presaged the oncoming storm,
Which quickly grew to rage its violence against the calmness
of our psyche.

Shrieking storm birds fled
The grimly smiling teeth of the assaulting sea
As again and again it crashed against the rocky cliff:
Powering, pounding, pulverising,
Smashing, striking, splintering,
Grinding its rasping force
Against the weaknesses of its victims:
Insidiously disintegrating
A thousand million years of innocent building.

But
It stopped.
The sun came forth
And gently dispelled the anger;
Calmed the fears and soothed the hurt:
Applying a healing balm to the searing wounds
Which gently began to heal
As the warm, golden light slowly spread.

Andrew Mullin

WET PLAYTIME

It's cold and raining hard outside
The sky is dark and grey,
I hate it when I hear the words
'Wet weather play today!'

I don't like comics and rotten old jigsaws
That I can't do although I've tried and tried,
I don't like keeping my voice to a whisper
I'd much rather shout with my friends outside!

I don't like how the classroom gets stuffy
The windows steam up and it starts to smell,
I don't like having to queue for the loos
I'm getting a headache and I don't feel well.

Maybe at dinner time the weather will brighten
Maybe we'll go outside to play,
I'm praying for the bell to ring
So wet weather games can be packed away.

G Jill Todd

QUAKE, RATTLE 'N' ROLL

'Did the earth move for you my love?'
my hubby said to me
That was after we made love
the other night, you see.

As our bed it was a-shakin'
on the Richter scale 5.8
'Oh, let's try that again,' I said
'cos that was really great!'

Then I realised it was not
the only thing that was shakin'
The whole darn house was rattlin' too
an' that was no mistakin'

Panickin' I rolled out of bed
and ran into the night
Forgettin' that I had nought on
an' that's not a pretty sight!

The quake didn't last for very long
it came and went without warnin'
When it was safe I went back inside
an' found my hubby in bed snorin'

I thought the quake was really quite strong
thinkin' my maker, I thought I'd met
But I survived to tell the tale
of a night I shan't forget!

Pat Thoume

BUS STOPS AND PAVEMENTS

To the end of the world and back.
I didn't understand that.
Broken and shattered, splintered and torn, blinkered and drawn.
I've turned my life upside down. What was I doing?
It wasn't just me, my family as well.
Was it a cycle of events, or a plan well drawn?
Who knows when it hits, what the hurricane's towing?
Hits you in the head and leaves you broken.
I'm standing here at the bus stop waiting. No car, no house,
Just my legs to take me.
When the hurricane hits, it sure does take me.
When the hurricane hits, it sure does break me.
This is the closest I've come to my destination
But I'm not getting off, no, not at this station.

Andy Alison

BLIND

When we say, 'Blind'
What comes to your head?
An old joyless man,
Is that what comes to mind?

But is that really the truth?
When we think deep down and hard?
Is this blindness such a tragedy?
Is a blind man's life so scarred?

When we think what we see in the world;
The pain in a victim's eyes,
A war emerging from peace,
Deceit, disloyalty and lies.

Is it really that bad,
Not to be able to see all this,
Not to be poisoned by these sights?
Is it such a great fee?

The blind man can still hear a voice,
The laughter of a child,
He can smell a sweet red rose,
So scented and mild.

Can still touch the cheek
Of one so dear,
Can still hear the seas rushing
When strolling along a pier.

So when we say, 'Blind,'
What comes to your head?
An old, content man
Is what should come to mind.

Eloisa Rowland (13)

ODE TO THE GAS MAN

I sit alone thinking,
put on the gas fire;
It's too hot try the central heating.
Do I feel odd because of the gas? Does it leave an odour, when on?
They tell me it's safe, they have for years,
To allay my fears.
I hope they're right, for me it would bring tears.
I have to believe them
My life is in their hands, for when it's cold,
I then feel bold. Switch it on!
And hope for the best, then sit back, and let them do the rest.

Elaine Backham

THE WOBBLY TOOTH

I am the tooth
That is in your mouth
No one knows
When I will come out

I get wobbled and wobbled
Pushed about
Is it no wonder
That I will come out?

The child is making a terrible mistake
I am starting to get mean
I watched the child as he put the
Money into the vending machine

Out came some chewy sweets
The child opened the pack
I popped out of the gum
With a mighty big crack

The child felt something hard in their mouth
They spat it on the ground
And there I was the wobbly tooth
No one made a sound

That night I was put under a pillow
But at least I was safe
And now the tooth fairy will come
And take me to a better place

Matthew Griffin

DEATH

His pale white face, as cold red blood drips down,
His eyes wide open and his mouth firmly frowned,
Just a simple gold wedding band,
Neatly placed on his dirty left hand,
A hand gently held to his chest,
As he lay there put to rest,
I close my eyes I can't bare to look,
I try not to think of the pain this poor man must have took,
I sat down and began to wonder why,
Why this murdered victim deserved to die,
What do we tell his distraught family?
Maybe now he's where he's meant to be,
To bring a new life into the world is so quick,
To take it out for no reason makes me feel sick,
This man has no chance not now,
We don't know why and we don't know how,
One single bullet through his head,
Now this poor man's lying dead.

Anita Masters

GOING POTTY

There was something funny on the news today.
Some clever scientists felt they just had to say
That smoking cannabis was bad for you in so many ways.
Lung and liver disease, and insanity too,
I'm sure they can't have thought this through,
Just look at it from my point of view.
For now it seems clear to me that
in any future mitigation all I will have to say is -
'I'm so sorry M'lud, Ladies and Gentlemen,
I must admit to having smoked too much Pot
And had, therefore, temporarily,
Completely lost the plot!'

Christine Bennett

APOCRYPHAL APPLE

First the momentary eclipse - then the dazzling
stars assort in the twinkle of a vision - probing

expansion to mystical knowledge - 'to boldly go
where no man has gone before' - as if Indiana Jones

boarded USS Enterprise to seek The Holy Grail - beyond frontier
a universal throb is metronome to cosmic harmony

if you integrate: planetary mechanics - barber-shop axles
humming to the stringencies of a Kepler Libretto

with Galileo's galactic postulate- an opera starring
    The Sun -

(a red-rag differential that attracted
Papal Bull - mandating repulsion
on an invoice stamped: *Heresy*
and the world went on spinning
its spin as the sun showed up shiny and bright, fresh as a daisy
each new morn and the moon beamed its tidings
from dusk till dawn.)

as a Cox's Pippin fell
under the spell of *gravity,* plummeting

a trajectory with ricocheting integrity: its ballistics
playing midwife to holistic gravitation theory.

Go see for yourself - the tree is still there.

Rona Scott

WOODEN NEW GUINEA GOD

From the front, I pause to take you in - perplexed,
misshapen idol with head lumped on ill-proportioned
body, the snip of your penis just a tapering twig,
as if you have nothing of manhood to prove. From

behind, the crack that split your back is bared
to view. Was this the blow that finally
disproved you, rendered you mortal, and bled
your people weak enough for mine to steal you?

I'd like to think so. As I circle your case, noting
every fault, like an officer around a new conscript,
your face is fixed so tight in fear I can almost
hear it splinter with the strain.

But is it fear? You have no eyes with which to be afraid -
just crude-cut overhangs, bleak and primitive, jutting
shadows - the only pools of shade in all your frame
that the strip-lights leave unplundered. From the side,

you look old and broken, a hacked tree stump
with holes in your cheek, and scars that run deep
in the grain of your wood. Your face is an abstraction,
and your body, propped rigid behind glass, a humiliation -

severed from the tribe that bears your image, severed
from the ones who carved you in theirs. You are hardened now,
dead wood - the timber petrified in the lines of your face,
frozen. Is this fear? I'd like to think so.

Nick Hunt

VISION

I have options,
I told him to his face.

Short-sighted in one eye, and long sighted in the other,
I have options.
I wink and the world changes
and when I look straight ahead, I have a mix of both.

Don't they cancel each other out?
he asks, and I wonder how I will make him understand.

I can choose to see you clearly,
or as a silhouette,
or not at all,
with a wink.
I can reshape my world, with a wink.

Misinterpreting,
people wave and smile and ask me if I'd like a drink,
or they sympathise with my nervous disposition,
but I am merely choosing what I see.
I have options.

He stares at me for a while
with his twenty-twenty vision.

Have you thought of glasses? he asks.
I blink my reply.

Fi Benson

DRUGS

She does not rush, what is haste?
Her hair is crumpled, her face, white paste.
Dark glasses shade the twinkling light.
Day must not conquer the black of night.

Twenty-eight or twenty-nine,
No difference really, what is time?
I speak to her, but she's not there.
She does not answer, she does not care.

Tomorrow's so distant, there's no yesterday.
Existence, an effort to make day by day.
The downfall of life, etched there on her arm,
Where drug-filled needles brought on this harm.

But she was once the sparkle at dawn.
God blessed the day that she was born.
Her father's darling, her siblings' best friend.
From a house full of love, to this terrible end.

My pride and joy, when she sang for her school,
And took first prize for standards and rules.
But a mother's love will never cease.
She's always my daughter, every drug ridden piece.

Mary E Allen

OPERATION BASIN

They had warned her they would come,
yet still their arrival seemed sudden.
Her heart began to pound uncontrollably
and beads of perspiration began to form on her forehead
and across her upper lip.
She really did not want to do this, but knew she must.
She had no choice.
Two encouraging but firm hands either side of her
were already helping her to her feet,
there would be no turning back.
Panic seized her and the pain was overwhelming,
its effect more intoxicating than five best malt whiskies straight down.
She positively floated.
'Come on - you're doing fine,' and the grip tightened
under her arms. First foot forward.
'One small step for man, one giant leap for mankind.'
Yes, it surely rated up there,
somewhere up there.
'Good, come on, another,' and there was no lingering.
A second step, and jubilation.
'Nearly there,' and a third was underway. She had done it!
She had done it!
Legs like jelly, practically detached.
A confusion of shuffling and congratulatory hugs, and she
hardly noticed the return trip at all.
Just the ecstatic relief of lying back on soft pillows, triumphant.

Now they would let her rest. It was over.
She had walked those first three important steps
from her bed to the washbasin.
Tomorrow she would walk to the door.

Julie Holness

DID YOU HEAR THAT?

Did you hear that?
I heard a creak in the floor
What could it be?
Maybe a ferocious monster has come to scare me
Listen, there it is again
Did you feel that?
I felt something brush past me
Maybe a brave lion is preparing itself to pounce on me
What are you laughing at?
It is not funny this is a serious matter
We could be brainwashed by intelligent aliens
This could scar us for the rest of our lives
I will never be able to go to college or get my first job
I will never be able to marry the woman of my dreams and
Hold my firstborn child in my arms
But worst of all, I will never be able to watch another
episode of EastEnders ever again!
What are you doing?
You can't go to sleep, there is something in this room.
Alright, maybe you're right, maybe there is nothing in the room.
Maybe I am just being paranoid.
Wait listen . . .
Did you hear that?

Lauren Williamson

ILL MET BY MOONLIGHT

Shadows shifting, shadow swift
Mothwings bathed in moonlight drift
Woodland creature stir in sleep
Forest secrets, buried deep
In the hushed, hallowed hour before dawn
By a pool of liquid night
Deep in shade, half-hid from sight
There, you watched, expectantly
Star-flecked eyes affixed on me
Was it you I met there, Titania
In the awesome, silent stillness before dawn?
There I stood, lost and helpless
Held in thrall, hypnotised
Bewitched by your glamour
By the fatal, faery magic in your eyes
Then the shadows retreated
And birds of day took flight
And your eyes lost their glimmer
As the sky grew bright
One last fleeting glimpse
As you faded from my sight
And all in a moment, you were gone
Like a dream, you vanished
Like a phantom, you were banished
By the cold, clear crystal light of dawn

Leyna Brinkmeyer

THREE SCHEMING SISTERS

'Go Away!' . . .
Threatens the one who spies me glance in her direction.
Had she not -
I wouldn't have noticed,
The three of them there at all.
So lingering not, I hurried away
From their curiously cold commotion . . .

'He'll pay for this, he'll pay for that!
We'll fill him full of poison . . .
And when he's dead, he'll be as bread
For the crabs out in the ocean.'

Ken Pope

THE FOLLOWER

As I walk along the deserted street,
A sudden thought grips my attention,
'There's someone following me.'
My heart rate quickens in time with my speeded steps.
My destination seems so far away
As there is no one to offer help.
I concentrate on moving fast,
But I cannot widen the gap between myself and my oppressor.
The faster I run, the faster they run.
I can sense their presence behind.
My situation is hopeless.
I must admit defeat,
I can only turn round and face my fate.
On doing so, I discover no one,
I see nothing to resemble a person except my shadow,
Which mockingly imitates my movements
In the deserted street.

Sharon Ferguson

SELENE

Of that pale moon I dream
watching her gentle light.
It's darker in the woods at night
I fear the sounds that creep.
Small feet
eyes glowing in the trees,
Owls hoot that signal death.

The fire grows weak,
my mind weaker.

What terror will come;
should I probe the future
look for my fate?
Alone in the dark forest
like a beast I feel wild
I sense a presence drawing in.

A cold chill wraps its arms
hugs me without comfort.

Sparks rise and I watch their passage;
I wish to know the moon's secret,
yet I struggle with fear.
'Selene' I whisper, and peer into her glow
all I want is to know,
then her truth touches me
as the sounds draw in.

Alan J Hedgecock

MADNESS

The corridor was Dark.
In the middle of it - a Shark!

In its mouth was a Phone.
Which was hired out - on loan!

The dialling tone - it spoke.
And I began to choke!

And Awoke!

To find myself Alone.
Deafened by my moan!

Imprisoned by the Light.
As it fell on padded White!

I twisted round - and fell.

In my Padded Cell!

Simon P Wilkinson

POTATOES

Come November, I am reminded
Of going to the garage
In the dark
For potatoes.

The sack sat near the door
Shrouded in shadows.
There was never enough light
Cast from the kitchen
To quiet my nerves.

My tentative hand would seek
The large, cold spuds,
Discarding the small ones,
Gathering enough for the five of us.

I always feared sudden movements
Under my hand,
Warmth or fur,
A mouse.
Or worse.

For company in there
On those dark evenings,
Ten feet from the safe haven
Of mince and onion, frying
I had the cold, damp smell
Of my own fear.

Jo Leak

THERE'S NOTHING THERE?

Last night, and through my inner ear,
I tried to listen, but could not hear
That sound. A noise which through the night,
Had scared and filled me full of fright.

Did I hear, or did I miss
The lowly rumble, the silent hiss.
That serpent, entangled in my brain
And now I lay here once again.

My eyes grow weary, there's nothing there
But the black of darkness, yet do they care?
Those evil terrors have come again,
To haunt and taunt and cause me pain.

It's there once more. I strain to hear.
Then shout out loud, 'You're not out there,'
Hoping against hope, they'll go away,
And knowing they will, come the light of day.

But now I lay quaking, upon my bed,
Could these be calls from all those long dead?
Then strain my ears to hear that sound,
The one that's not there, yet all around.

Richard Lee Nettleton

NOT HAUNTED

There's a shadow on the curtain
Where no tree casts its shape
There's a creaking in the passage
Where no foot drops its weight
There's a stain upon a wall
Where no damp should be spread
There's a whisper in the garden
Where no visitor is seen
There's a scent within a chamber
Where no lady has sat
There's a disturbance in the dust
Where no finger has traced
There's a chill beside the fire
Where draft is never felt
There's a churning in my gut
Where no guilt should be.

Cardinal Cox

WHAT THE SKELETON SAYS

Do not be afraid.
Be aware of my raw beauty inside you -
Solidity of skull, slenderness of finger,
Toughness and smoothness of textures,
Strength of spine, power of pelvis,
Firmness of feet, flexibility of joint.

Wave your arms in the wind.
Swivel your head to catch the flight of a swallow.
Bend the back and flex the knee
To dig deep into the fertile earth.
Kneel in prayer under a summer sky
Or, in the depth of winter, to touch the first snowdrop.

You are a child again
Discovering the miracle of movement,
Jumping over rock pools,
Swimming naked through the long grass.

Do not be afraid.
I am the bringer of joy and fulfilment.

I am the last dancer.
My song is the percussion of bones.
Round the lines and curves of my frame
Space is flowing.
Soon I shall be invisible, intangible.
I shall be dancing with God.

Chris Woodland

FREE MORNING, FREE ...

In the grey of the sun split morning,
when the wind crashes the street plan trees
you can walk through an eternity of stubbled fields,
knowing only your tossing hair
and your mud-weighed shoes
and you are nobody
and you belong to nobody
and you are complete and entirely alone.

Your thoughts and worries now are unconnected
and the cog-wheels of your mind are spinning free;
so free that when, in the distance,
a blackbird cries and breaks through the wind,
you are at one with him.

This time is timeless
and this freedom is the freedom
that belongs to all the world.

Ian Fearnside

ALL ALONE

Nowhere to go now
Nothing to do but sit alone
And think of you
The days are shorter
The nights are so long
I sit and wonder all alone
How we talked and
How we played
On those lazy summer days
Now all over
Here again
Sat on my own going insane
So I'll wonder what went wrong and
Why you left and never came home.

Karen Foxall

ANCIENT RECORDS, LAID OUT

Focus, guided by the heavens, on
Plains of enlightenment, still, quiet, the
Lines go right through, lit by the stars.
Quietly, amid richness and connection
Here is the weirdness to analyse.

Michael Courtney Soper

THAT NIGHT IN THE LANTERN GRILL

That night in the Lantern Grill,
Seated low, two figures,
By candlelight they swithered,
Playing chess with the salt
And pepper pots, I figured,
That night in the Lantern Grill.

Their shadows danced
And slithered, as the candles
Spluttered and flickered,
That night in the Lantern Grill.

Well after moonset
They dithered,
Those two in the Lantern Grill -
And as the last chimes of midnight
Withered, the end-game finalised,
I twiggered,
That night in the Lantern Grill.

Terrence St John

THE STATE OF GRACE

Falling was riotous for Grace
With her lapse of decorum,
she was happy in sin.

Ridiculously in love
at an age that missed passion,
she greedily hauled it in.

Taking bodily liberties that ask no account
she acted -
impurely - on a whim.

Taking love as it was offered,
tendering its currency,
she took him by the limb.

Taking the easy way,
valuing the face,
attached to the skin,

she subtracted her age
lightened her life,
held out her cap for the wind.

Sue Britchford

WITHIN THE VALLEY

Roses cut deep into your flesh,
within your wondrous luscious valley,
I beg to explore and reveal a river of sweet passion juice.
I declare to bestow upon you a life of joy beyond belief,
I send a message telepathically of the feelings I possess.

Rigid nails upon your body,
blooded wrists from restrained subjugation,
pleasure weeps from every oral cavity
in tears you howl sonnets of undying want.

Protect what thoughts are summoned between us
as our auras dance with no regret.

David Bilsborrow

CAPRICORN

I am the salt of the Earth,
I am the goat, who butts in,
I thirst for knowledge
And drink at the fountain of Youth.

I am open minded yet will
Argue my opinion for
I am always right in the end
I have an earthy sense of humour.

I am intensely loyal
To my loved ones and friends
I can command respect yet
I am a friend to humility.

I share my sign with madness
With genius too
Bowie, Presley, Jesus!
And if Jesus was a Capricorn then so is his dad.

As my birth sign dictates
I am one of two things:
Your sweetest dream or
Your darkest nightmare.

I can be the soul of the party
Or happy alone
Like the goat in my character
Sure-footed, ambitious and true.

Derek Blackburn

MY GOAT'S GREY EYES

My goat's grey eyes see the dustbin is open
To the still voice of the flowers:
It stands the shadow of the vale
When the sun has death's eagles upon its mane:

The rock is smiling upon the desert:
It sees the sword of night upon the camel's eyes
That journeys to the ocean
Of delight: the milk of apes is dried
In the ancient blood of the fly.

Edmund Saint George Mooney

How To Be A Mum!

So you'd like to be a hairdresser
A fighter pilot or a nun,
But the course I'm really looking for
Is 'How to be a mum'.
You don't receive any training
You're on a 'twenty-four hour' call,
You fit fifteen job descriptions
But there is no pay at all!
They only have to say 'I love you Mum'
To melt my heart away,
Doesn't seem to really matter now
That I was cross with them that day.
You love your children all to bits
But do you get respect?
Everyone's got the 'Kevin' attitude
So what do you *really* expect!
As I sit here inside this office room
With no diplomas or degrees,
'Well just what have you done then?'
The interviewer sneers at me
Well, I've been a nurse and a teacher
A chauffeur and a referee,
An agony aunt and a cleaner
And an accountant of the highest degree!
The house is very quiet now
The experts say it's 'Empty Nest'
But as I look at my grown up children now
I'm happy I achieved my very best!

Sheila Moore

BAMPTON COMMON

Daybreak tenderly caressed the surrounding coppice,
while jaded pigmented foliage, surrendered meekly
in favour of a gentle tawny hue.
From this elevated vantage point, the valley below,
took the resemblance of exquisitely crafted miniatures.
Their periphery succumbing to meadows
of multifarious colours, encapsulating the
outlying farms and smallholdings.
A flock of sheep drifts downwards, like a
swollen stream that cascades down a crevice.
Bleating, floating in air currents
meander incorrigibly, in time with rolling contours.

Melody from a nearby Linnet, reverberated, like a cadenza,
and, as others joined the throng, the resonance intensified
to a harmonious crescendo, sheer pleasure unrivalled.
On such a morning, beauty and splendour walk hand in hand.
Below, ramblers depart for an early morning hike, pushing
through the grass, sending diminutive droplets of dew down towards
Mother Earth, only to be absorbed, and never seen again.
Chapel bells toll from a nearby parish.
Worshippers congregate, heads held high, anticipation fills the air.
A view point such as this is much sought,
many have tried, most have failed, nature declared
arms to be wings, the power of flight.

Dave Wilton

NEW BABY JOYS

Still the clamour of the starlight,
Stop the noisy moonbeams fall.
Catch the leaves in glade and woodland,
Keep the silence over all.
. . . our baby sleeps.

Watch in wonder long dark lashes
Resting on her shell pink cheeks.
Rosebud mouth in sweet perfection
Gently smiling as she sleeps.
. . . our baby dreams.

Tell the birds to wake the morning.
Hear the golden sunbeams sing.
Dancing daylight shouts with gladness,
Across the land let church bells ring.
. . . our baby awakes!

Ann Kelley

AND SOMETIMES A MIRROR

Some people you just can't reach
They will never learn but can always preach
They exist in such a closed mind state
When their eyes become blinkered then it's too late
They are way beyond your outstretched hand
They live in a world only they understand
Paranoia lurks around every bend
They see no reason to change or mend
They are so caught up in their own little net
Their thoughts are for them and as far as they get
They cannot see in wider view
There is only them and never you
They will not believe that others care
It's the world against them and nothing is fair
They have no concern for those they know
Who suffer the brunt of the paranoid blows
Nothing registers that may cause pain
It is everyone else that is always to blame
Their wall is building higher each day
And nothing else matters except what they say

Is there a solution or some way in?
To break down the barriers and begin
To change the mind and open the eyes
To silence the sound of a heart that cries

Dave Palmer

AWAITED SCENARIO

A face of anguish,
Host of all souls,
A face of expression,
Experience of blows,
A one night of psychotic behaviour,
Of destroyance,
Pray our saviour,
A long wide tunnel,
Searching in vain,
A bright light ahead,
Down that long dreary lane.

Chloe Davies

DAY-DREAM

Laying on the hearth-rug,
Dark Jamaican in my hand
I gazed up at the portrait
Of the warm Barbados sand;
It took but only seconds
E're I could smell the breeze,
Coming from the ocean,
Rustling through the trees;
My body gently swaying to
The rhythm I could feel,
From the happy Native band
With drums of British steel.
I smelt the sweet hibiscus
And the Bougainvillaea bloom,
As the breeze blew on the pollen
Spreading all around the room.
I longed to hurl my body, deep,
Within the deep blue sea,
To scuba, to the old wreck
That had fascinated me;
Alas, my glass now empty,
My body back again,
Laid upon the hearth-rug,
Yet, my mind still held the train
Of thought, which was a daydream
That chased away the grey
Of the curse, that lies o'er Britain
On a dark November day.

Les Hanson

IF ONLY

I've been doing some serious thinking
And the think I don't need in my life
Is a helpless incompetent husband?
How I wish that I'd married a wife

Someone to turn *me* out neatly
To ensure that *my* blouses are pressed
I'm late home, he simply smiles sweetly
Saying 'Darling sit down, you look stressed.

I'll massage your tired aching shoulders
Here's your supper; it's still piping hot
I'll pour you a large gin and tonic
Oh, I've paid all those bills you forgot.'

It's so hard to stop myself screaming
When he asks 'What's this mess on the floor?'
Walks over it, picks up his paper
Assuming I'll clean it for sure.

I arrive home; he smiles at me smugly
'Brought your washing in - only in time'
I wonder where are *his* items
Still hanging there, limp on the line?

'Oh, that appointment, remind me tomorrow
And when was our holiday planned?
Did you arrange for the car and gas man?
Can you pay the credit card final demand?'

Yet *my* job is equally stressful
My hours are equally long
We both leave at eight every morning
And get home at six - what went wrong!

Madeleine Reid

BE HAPPY

Smile, don't frown, laugh don't cry,
don't let happiness pass you by,
life is full of gloom and sorrow,
always believe it will be better tomorrow.

And when the sun shines on a brand new day,
be glad that the old one has gone away,
for if you always look for the good side of life,
then you will be free from trouble and strife.

Stand up and take a look around,
happiness is there, waiting to be found.

Gaellen

NIGHT OF THE FOX

The dishes which had nattered for attention all evening
fell silent in my hands.
A lean and shaggy outline he stepped delicately
about the lawn in front of the old people's home.
Repeatedly dipping his head to the neon grass
as the lights from the building found the lights in his coat.
Hunting for worms I guessed.
He moved carefully but with a surprising boldness.
He knew the territory.
So close to the sleeping and so alienated.
I met him once in broad daylight.
Coming upon him suddenly in rough ground where the garden stopped.
We stood rock still and stared at each other.
He had seemed to be waiting for something.
As though he associated me with the leftover chicken and cheap
sardines anonymously offered in secret places
where no dog could find them.
Watching him now from my kitchen window
I moved cautiously for a better view.
He looked up as though hearkening to a call
and stared directly at me.
Then he reared and glowing in the lights
rubbed his shoulder against a tree in the manner of a domestic cat.
Once, twice, three times before turning away
to become part of the shrubbery.
I called out but did not speak.
No hurt in all the Holy Mountain.
The neon bright night saw and heard nothing
of my babble.

Marjorie Green

A LIVING ROOT

Firmly rooted in the ground,
I lay here deeply,
Not a sound.
I feed and flourish
And grow inside,
Content in my role,
As life I provide.
I have strength, courage
And love to offer,
Yet wish from this,
Nothing to proffer.
But sometimes I need,
A helping hand,
To be nurtured too,
You understand.

Sue Umanski

DRAGONFLY

Dragonfly of azure blue
The gentlest touch on my finger
I am honoured that you have alighted on me
Grateful for the gift of your presence
While you take your rest, soaking up the sun
So that once again you can take to the skies

I watch you, barely daring to breathe
So scared that you will fly too soon
Your wings are so delicate; perfection itself
A study in blackwork and symmetry
Surely stitched by the Goddess herself
On a quiet, peaceful evening when she was alone

I blink; too late, you are gone!
All of a sudden you have flown away
I watch you glide, soaring on the currents of air
As they lift and support you on your flight
My gaze follows your path through the air
I feel bereft and alone once more; missing your companionship

I wonder if you realise how fortunate you are
To be so free, to be able to fly
For you, no feet of clay, no earthbound gravity
To hold you down, to keep you trapped
Escape; fly free my friend, kiss the air for me
I shall remember you and the gift you gave to me

Heide Lhotka

WHY?

Why does the world lie?
Why do we have to die?
Why does the sun shine?
Why not always darkness?

Why do we have to live,
Through pain and misery?
Why is it that when we die,
We go through it eternally?

Why does time go by?
Why can't people fly?
Why do seasons change?
Why can't things stay the same?

Why do we have to live,
When the world is hateful?
Why is it when close ones die,
The procedure is so painful?

Helen-Elaine Oliver (14)

SOLITUDE BRINGS FREEDOM

In solitude I sit wondering why?
What am I doing in this place?
Having time to think is soothing to my mind
Can you see it on my face?
All day I listen to others
With their aches and pains and moans
Giving my ear and my time
It's heaven to be alone
People may think I am lonely
Because I sit alone
Am I deemed to be eccentric?
I just want to be on my own
All that matters is that I am
What I want to be
Free of worry and of pain
Just happy being free.

Robert Salter

THE TIGHT ROPE

Sometimes, like a kite on a taut string, my soul sings . . .
Listen:

In sudden leaps of flaming sound
That catch the truth before it bounds
Away to tight-ropes high as hell
Where spirit-clowns are tip-toeing
And laughing at the ones who fell
Ah! laughing at the ones who fell
Laughing at death, my spirit clowns . . .
Above the picture-postcard towns
They fly, impossibly dancing
On air as high as hell.

And where the mirror-mind reflects'
There where the tight-rope intersects
What's real from our imaginings,
Over the perfect precipice
They leap, mocking the need for wings;
Mocking the need for anything
They fly, flaunting their beauty, wild.
With joy I follow like a child
Not caring if they kill or kiss;
I have to risk this thing . . .

And later, in the dead of night
Bathed in the moon's marmoreal light
They play with shadows for a change,
Moving their fingers cunningly
To see the patterns re-arrange;
The shadow-creatures shift and change . . .
So that a child, tired from the day
Dreams as the shadow-beings play
And someone somewhere calls for me
From far away . . . how strange.

There: with my wild imaginings;
There: following the faint smoke-rings;
There: high above the kestrel's wings;
There: where the wind stings;
There;
There!
My soul sings . . .
Like a kite on a taut string,
My soul sings!

Chris Glassfield

AMOUR OR LESS

His vision will go shrining for her face
In crowd street bustles, in yawning spaces
Where she is, where she once was
And where she can never be

She will dance alone on paths that only she sees
And gesture him not to follow
Knowing in his nature that he must

Infrequently to amazement she will gift him
And laugh his responses into sallies of forgiving
Weighted counterpoints of forgetfulness

Sloughing, inventive he will sing
And she must give an account of listening
To the things she can never hear

Tender in regret
In the passion-bower of his soul, he will make a bed for her
There to kiss her eyelids into absolutions of sleep

Here as daylight insists
She will smile him out of sense
Out of time and out of all argument

She will bring sweet confusion
Unconscionably stealing himself
And he will thank her for it

All in all
She will show him nothing of herself
And in gratitude

He will gaze at it forever

David Bower

TIP OF MY FINGER

Close your eyes and hold your tongue.
Feel my fingers talk, telling you all you need to know.
On the tip of each finger, you'll find more answers than on the
Tip of my tongue.

Words have little action,
Although they may move you.
They have too many meanings, there are too many of them.
See, I have only ten fingers, five on each hand.
And one would say enough to last you the night.

Jane Terry

FINDING WITHIN

Search deep inside, what do you hide
but what are you really trying to find?
An inhibition from in your soul,
you're looking far beyond,
Pull back the layers, one by one,
study each, like a page.
The inspiration that you will seek does
not come from others, nor genetic from our mothers.
Don't hide away and bring on tension
just go out and find a new intervention.
A journey on life's paths will show
where others surely follow,
They walk around within this world they tread the land
thinking life's love is so bland.
Whilst give and take from the other hand,
cast your net then reel it in,
You will never know what is within.
Just go forth, turn up a challenge,
overcome these simple tasks.
You have found yourself at last.

Karl Bradshaw-White

WORK OF ART

It is tenth of June, 2000.
I am working on four big canvasses,
I may die during the night,
It wouldn't bother me.
I have covered the first canvas - leave to dry.
Tomorrow (Saturday) I start another.
4ft by 6.
Exeter last Monday, bought palate knife and brushes.
It is 1.45 Saturday morning, I am listening to
Mini-disc on the headphones,
Thinking about sex and drawing.

Fergus Hilton

UNTITLED

A faint light shimmers against a vast darkness,
The black blanket enhances the defined shape,
Whilst almost losing the image forever,
It is there, though mostly hidden from life.

The light of day and reality disguises its existence,
It becomes forgotten by the world until dark,
Even when it shivers in the coldness of night,
It remains an undistinguished blur to all.

Barely noticed among the thousands of other lights,
A hope which lies within, but is never fulfilled,
Just another face in the crowd, with no name,
An unnecessary addition to this place known as life.

The prison of night is so cold, too dark to survive,
Escape is impossible from the constant torment.
A chance for freedom is craved and yearned for,
Whilst desperation destroys all links to the future.

People look on in awe, at the superficial sight,
Exclamations of delight mean nothing for long,
It is too far away, untouchable by everyone,
The light slowly fades, as the sun rises high,
And the star soon appears to be nothing at all.

Amanda Friend

AIR TIME

we never sit
and stare at
the walls
these days,
the paper
has got
old and sore

now
we don't
try so hard,
watching
television far
into sleep

I used to hate
to hear
hellfire
and salvation,
and tanks
and red underwear
and UFOs
all night
and dawn

now we
keep them
in the pipes
and when we
yawn
we struggle
for air
time

Ian Bishop

UNTITLED

I will drive the
Cadillac of desire
down the streets of fear
And park outside
the garden of Eden.
Give the keys
to the putti valets
and open the gate.
The fragrances
of hope will meet
me and my senses
will overload on
pure truth.
I will feel good
never better
I will feel like
I finally have
known myself
as others know me.
My enemies will
stand in line
waiting to shake
my hand
I will make amends
and burn my ego
on the bonfire
of vanity

And standing there
with no need of
garment or shoes
no call for speech
and no way to
communicate
will finally be
at rest.

Tony Lundop

SHACKLES

Would you now mourn
the Burka of woman
and shackles worn be worn,
to never more clink beneath
the treaded sand of sisters adorn.

Let this death sleep when
you, thrice faceted, come into
sight of this. See again
where it lies, so stooped like
weighted back, barrowing again.

Without a cent nor sense for doubt,
the footing of this female mind,
set by female hands, without
worthies would-be, placed ever-solid
as infallible wont about.

And would you become
the dressing of war, forget
fight and bloody scorn, run
no more the chimera, nor succumb
and let these heathen vice be done.

Not cussing chide nor bodice tie,
not bluff nor love deny,
whisper ye words upon hate and love
and breathe them life for years to come . . .

Caoilinn Hughes

SILENT TEARS

Many are we
who weep in vain
the silent tears
the aching heart
on pillow slip
soft falling rain
for dreams of love
that seem obscure
the passing years
the wish so pure
material wealth
to some may be
for happiness a necessity
he who desires
a deeper bond
a path of souls
that leads beyond
seek longer still
till fate decides
what washes in
on new spring tides.

Ann M Pilcher

EPIPHANY

The star drove me on inexorably.
From the beginning my mind was fixed
Upon the Word, although the star I followed
Was often distant, elusive, even hidden.
The light of many days nullified it:
Stargazers need the night.
But my days were joyful, bright
And full of the light no star could penetrate.
The journey, I knew, would be a long one.

I visited the palaces
Of other people's minds:
Aeons of experience and imagination
Encapsulated between many covers.
I sought the help of the great of all the ages,
But never forgot the star that was my guide,
The burning within me.
I journeyed on in vague, haphazard fashion
Always reaching out for that which was beyond,
Catching, from time to time,
Some gleam of starlight
To spur me on.

The revelation, when it came,
Was not as I expected it.
In some far future
Let Saul see light on some Damascus road:
For me it was a quiet, gentle sense
As of a god coming from out the gloom
In a place of no consequence,
Yet full of power and all-empowering.

I felt as if my gifts were stripped from me,
Accepted and transformed, returned again.
I not the visitor, the traveller,
As I supposed: I the recipient
Of gifts beyond the gifts that I had given:
The subject of some mystic Visitation.
It was as if I dreamed a dream,
Took note, obeyed, did not retrace my steps,
But turned for home, the purpose of my life
Accomplished.

Returned another way.

Pam Gidney

TOURIST TRAP

I watch with tears . . . As shifting shapeless shadows caress
her ebon breasts. Tonight, as for a million years.

Whence her dark volcanic form,
Body blessed of countless secret clefts,
Heaved then in writhen passion beneath a seething ocean storm.

The curtaining, cumulus cowl bedims her brazen buttes,
Cascades her craggy cliffs. As I sigh . . .

Once eclipsed, the seaward cloud, unveils a lucent moon
lofty mistress to a diamond encrusted sky.
Lays bare her landscape raw.

Lime-washed dwellings lustrous as pearls,
Unstrung aside a surf-laced Neptune shore.

I whisper. To pleasure my ears. Jealous of my eyes.
    'Enthralling. Elysium exemplified!'

Soft words spin about my head. Pilfered from my lips
as the sultry sea-borne breeze rustles as a rare palm.

Idyll lost to eternity as the distant atonal clangour,
of goat bells, is cantored by a cockerel's raucous cry.

Impatient for the dawn I so dread.
So near, so calm. Her summit stretching skyward.
Sensuous shoulders bearing verdant valleys to a lazily lapping Atlantic;
Proud womb to such ageless splendour.

Sad siren, who has seduced us so, to do our worst;
Pride is *yours,* a stir of Nature,
Who knew not the curse of Man's contempt.

As my heavy footsteps defile the virgin sand, I wish
this were Man's vilest crime against this fair Canary Isle,
For the clement surf will absolve me this.

But tide nor time can condone the malignant curse
we have dealt this once peaceful place of untold bliss.
Nor any god, forgive us, the 'packaged' rape of 'Atlantis'.

Colm Brook-Gibbs

SOUTHEND BANK HOLIDAY

Milling thronging coloured ants
Swarming everywhere,
Rushing, jostling, pushing, staring,
Not an inch to spare.
Queuing, eating, drinking, licking
Whatever is their pleasure,
Laden pushchairs spilling out
Some parent's little treasure.
Screams from teenagers on wheel,
Is it really safe?
Never mind when ride is over
Make for nearest cafe.
Hot dogs, burgers, donuts, coke
Who cares what they eat?
It's bank holiday, let's enjoy it
Everything's a treat.
When the day is nearly over
Weary feet are homeward bound,
Bleary eyed and sticky-fingered
Make for car or train.
Snogging couples linger longer
Parting is a pain,
When next holiday comes around
Start it all again!

Gwen Place

I HAVE . . .

I have lain on mountain sides,
Wind in bracken sighing.
Gazed across restless seas
Watching fishes flying.
I have walked the ploughman's wake,
Spud picking, 'til my back ached.
I have strolled by hilly streams,
Dreaming dreams.

I have seen lambs dance in spring,
Guardian sheep dogs eyeing.
I have seen sheep block the roads
Welsh villagers defying.
I ran errands here and there,
Fetched hot bread from baker's lair.
I have roamed in city streets
Begging treats.
(Got any gum, chum?)

Working man at fourteen years
Twenty-four shillings earning.
National Service in Egypt's land -
Leave in Cyprus, swimming.
Shared my laughter, sang my song.
Tried to do what's right, not wrong.
Leaves me with so much to share,
If I dare.

Geoff Gaskill

WISH A WISH

When I was young I was told it was wrong to wish a wish,
To be able to wish to have power to heal and create was
something we all couldn't have,
But as you grow in age you feel the wish in you,
You feel it growing with you, with your thoughts and ways.
So sometime in your life you will realise you had the power all along,
Inside you and all it needed was a little kick.
And as you grow you realise along with your power that the person
whom told you it was wrong to wish a wish wasn't being uncreative,
they were simply telling you, you don't need to wish a wish,
To have power to heal and create.

Lisha Naomi Binns

AN ODE TO AN 'UNFIT HOUSE'

Hands off my house . . ! There isn't a mouse to be seen
And it's perfectly clean.
Not a bat nor a slug, not a rat nor a bug,
No fleas or lice . . . 'In fact quite nice!'

I've nothing to fear, the passage is clear,
The staircase free with a handrail for me.
I add with pride the toilets inside and
Fresh air comes and goes as it pleases.

The kitchen is ample for any cordon bleu sample,
With cupboards galore my provisions to store.
I emphatically say light is good thro' the day,
Waste water's no strain it flows down the drain.

There's no rising damp in my little camp,
Not a crack nor a bulge in the walls,
No worm in the wood and the beams are good
Quite solid, not likely to fall.

There isn't a droop anywhere in the roof,
'The gutters and stack?' Well there's nothing they lack!
'The yard at the back,' beg pardon it's now a garden
I want you to know this describes the whole row.

'Now come . . ! Can you call this a slum?'

Florence Taylor

THE STALKER

Hairs standing up on the back of her neck,
Blood pounding in her veins,
Heart fluttering like a wild bird,
She once again felt she was going insane.

Each night this week, the same feeling had occurred.
Eyes on her back, steps matching hers,
Turning round to see darkness and isolation,
But certainty reigned - the wrong person stares.

She'd followed advice, varied her route,
Her usual amble, replaced with a stride.
Keys held in her hand, alarm in her pocket,
Middle of the road, less places to hide.

Slamming the door behind with a huge sigh of relief,
Waiting, leaning, heavily against the wood,
Ears straining to hear the sounds of the night,
Praying she was listening as hard as she could.

Long minutes pass and the threat finally wanes.
Door securely locked, she was safe at long last,
She doesn't know that he watches from outside,
That he's no stranger - just a 'friend' from her past.

Tracking the passage of lights through the house,
He settles to watch as she reaches her room.
Dark shadows abound, but they add to his mood,
Alone, dangerous and lost in the wintry gloom.

Time passes by, he's lost all count.
Cold to the bone, weary and sad,
He waits till he's sure she's really alone,
She was right when she left him, he really is mad.

Next night he follows her again. And every night since.
He misses her embraces, her laughter - wants to be back in her life,
Wants to hold her once again, to see her each night,
Not stalking her, spying on her, scaring her - his darling ex-wife.

Patricia Cunningham

A CALL FROM THE DOORWAY

A call from the doorway breaks my concentration,
the noise sounds like deprivation,
deprived of a human fed addiction.

A call from the doorway is a man of the street,
whose nameless figure sits bowed head
and seemingly subservient to people that pass.

A call from the doorway looks for the hand of charity
with the grace taken by the fault of past demons.

A call from the doorway works mind,
body and soul to a point of decision.
I feel cold, not bold as I walk the walk of shame.

Jonty Holt

CABBAGE PATCH

She bends over the cabbage field
The morning fog around.
Her frizzled black curls hang with dew.
She wields her surgeon's knife,
Cutting each orb of cabbage from its thick-set stem.

A modern 'Tess' she works her row
Black sweat upon her back; her orange trews
Proof against the wanton tractor which
Relentlessly collects box upon box.
Hour by hour. These will fill the citizens of town.

They know nothing of her toil,
The whims of sun and rain.
They drive into town in ordered line,
Read computers row by row
Sweating under neon lights in central heating.

At five o'clock they struggle home,
Pushing through traffic as in the morn.
Exhausted, they shower, eat and watch telly.
'Tess', rested from the midday heat,
Placidly cuts another row of cabbage in the evening air.

Jane England

THE OLD WOMAN

Help me please the old woman did say,
To me as I walked the other day.
I went to help, to try and see,
What I could do,
What was required of me?

She stood and took hold of my hand,
Her face, her complexion the colour of sand.
Take hold of these, take my load,
Please help me,
To cross this road.

I took the load, I did not complain.
Who she was I did not ascertain.
The traffic was busy in this section,
We travelled across,
I never made the connection.

When we were safe on the other side,
She took the load, and looked on with pride.
There is nothing in life you cannot achieve,
Just look, hope,
And truly believe.

She walked away, I know now where,
She had touched me and seemed to care.
I knew who my angel was indeed,
She would love and protect me,
That was guaranteed.

I strode away full of bliss,
Taken away from my dark abyss.
I take hold of my life I hold so dear,
But shall never forget,
Or ignore again, my fear.

Dawn Graham

COMMODITY

The metallic sound of the lift shaft echoes in his ears.
The clicking of high heels told him it was a woman.
As the sound grew fainter he tried to put a face to the sound,
But would he ever know if he was right?

Shortly afterwards the process was repeated,
Only this time squeaky crepe soles fuelled his pastime.

Invisible images of human life.
Faceless voices above and below him,
Laughter and chatter, but what did it matter?
His isolation exists right here:
No friendly face to say hello,
The milkman only knocks for his pay.

The flickering screen of the celluloid box in the corner caught his eye.
Images of material wealth flooded into the dingy sitting room.
Media hype, persuasive and desirable,
Gleaming cars on deserted roads, where tyres barely touch the dust.
While his eyes fell on his rusting bicycle standing in the narrow hall.
He saw his reflection on the screen and imagined,
Just for a moment that it was all within his reach.
Then, shrugging his shoulders he sat down at the Formica table
                                        and surveyed his estate.
Plastic sofa and Aunt Lily's sideboard,
The worn lino and unmatched wallpaper he had got from the sales.

Outside his flat, draughty corridors remain empty and bare.
Doors tightly closed against neighbourly invasion, like snails in retreat.
A concrete cocoon suspended in space with human beings
                                        stacked on shelves.
A commodity by themselves . . .

Pamela Murray

UNTITLED

Pillows and duvets are my landscapes for lonely picnics.
My own best friend and if I make it through this my own hero.
Faith in my own self religion has strayed like a confused
                                        homing pigeon.
Ground control to zero, bells ring but I'm not answering.
For death I'm practising, twelve hours during the day at least.
Comfort in the unconscious state of method decrease,
But thoughts hasten as I near form of awakened.
Two Kalms every four hours, two Nytol Herbal to be taken.
Twenty plus cigarettes to askew, my senses are aching.

Me to the side, low lighting on the event of sombre dwellings.
Thoughts bay viciously like agitated canines.
Complex entanglement of complicated sacrosanct.
Serenity is in the dust of summer garments from '89.
Onwards I march to my own metronome.
Gargoyles know me. I occasionally drift on a dream,
No further than what is seen in-between thin blue lines.
Pain threshold is battered and too old for all this.
Ignorance to the fact I'm losing self would be sublime.

M MacDonald

COME AND WALK WITH ME

Onward strolls the sea it cannot stop
as we stop to gaze. Align our eyes
with red. The rays of morning sky
sleeps on backs of waves.

Come and walk with me.
Your footprints shrink in shifting grains.
I know the future sands, I know the reams
of bays where dogs have run
and birds are blown
on draughty days where Sunday walks
and roasts
are memories. Come

and walk with me.
The ghost of moon moves above a relentless sea,
a watch-face watching
the seconds tick off your face. But now
our shuttered conversations with salty breaths
are locked inside the ears of shells beneath
the divers waves, beneath
the lighthouse sweep and sailor's bell.

M McCready

STAR

Hollow to the core,
A social whore.
Well fitting mask,
A bubbly laugh,
An icon to adore.

Hide from the daylight,
Blinds your rosy sight.
Comfort in crowds,
Say nothing loud,
Star that seeks spotlight.

Catherine Keenan

CIRCUMLOCUTION

Sunset
Nocturnal
Sunrise
Diurnal
Round 'n round
Orbicular
Tick
Tock
Rock 'n roll
All fall down
No one knows
Where to go
Tomorrow.
Never comes.

Girvin McBride

UNHAPPY MEAN

Life's a son of a bitch, pessimists will insist;
Daring to seem sexist, scorning to be PC.
Anyway, they say, the term is as much doggist
If you must examine every word's pedigree.
The canine link is *á propos* somehow,
To the cynics' legacy here and now.
Their dogged lineage runs back to classic time;
To Hebrews, Medes and Latins of a sophist mien.
An ancient seer, swathed in gear more suitable to bath in,
Easing his dodgy knees on a paillasse in Athens,
Devised the logic: sufficient, necessary and clear.
To all poor mortals Mother Nature at last appears
A hanging judge: cold, indifferent, without mercy.
So her brood must share her bloodhound's ferocity.

Owen Watson

REALISING

If it were money or love
What would a man choose?

The idiot with the money
Would try and buy it

When your child is born
Your fair home don't matter
Tripled stocks mean nothing

Are you in Heaven?
Something is being
And you have become

And ain't you proud
Dad!

The Psycho Poet

THE VISION

Braved against the elements
stands a weak and feeble form,
the white haired, aged Indian
looked fragile and forlorn
his arms extended upwards, his
face a mask of pain.
He seeks a vision for the people
to make them strong again.

Once more to roam this continent
once more to hunt and fish.
As one at peace with nature, red
brothers who walk this Earth.
No more the blue coat soldiers
no more their lies and scorn.
Just the gentle spirit of Mother Nature
smiling down on this her red
skinned sons.

Where once the Indian roamed
triumphant, no more they ride or trek
only rails of steel across their nation
and the iron horse rules the West.

Oh great spirit send me a vision
to set my people free.
Not prisoners on a reservation
full of hate, disease and fear.

But there is no hope for the poor Indian.
His triumphs they are no more,
only stories that are history
and the Indian's rotting bones.
Give a thought for the poor Indian,
for his story must be told.
The eternal spirit of America,
God bless their hearts and souls.

Gwyn Thomas

As Time Goes By

Where is the teddy I had
When I was one
Gone

Where is the doll I hugged
When I was ten
Vanished

Where is the pet I adored
When in my teens
Dead

Where is the boy I loved
When I was a girl
Lost

Where is the clock that ticked
All those years away,
Still here!

Maureen McMillan

THE SKY

A misty haze hangs over all
Sky a murky grey,
Not the best of mornings
To myself I say.

Suddenly a fiery glow
On horizon sweep,
Sunrise, breaking all
From their hazy sleep.

Gradually sky turns blue
With orange, golden streaks,
An awesome sight to be seen
From which each colour leaks.

Azure sky without a cloud
Its sunlight warm and bright,
Radiates a perfect day
Till sunset of the night.

Which is as spectacular
As the morning's glow,
Everything that we have seen
Is Nature's, fantastic show.

J Naylor

NEIL'S POEM

Hearts let loose to find their way
To wait
To wonder, come what may
Passing glances come and go
Will they touch love?
They don't know.

Stars in velvet heaven flicker and play
Bringing the end to a long, lonely day
Up above once again
Looking for a sign,
Something to gain.

Two hearts collide amongst shimmering star
Distance has no meaning,
No sense of how far.
Was it fate or just pure luck
From vast fields of wandering hearts
Each other's hearts we did pluck.

Life to be heard and to be told
Finding out what dreams they hold
The hopes
The fears
The love
The tears
Wishes and dreams for the coming years
Hearts like these are hard to find
Loving, giving
Warm and kind.

Vivien Hornidge

ANGEL OF FLAME

Everyone has their scars to hide
Some show a glimpse of this through child-like eyes
They stare with disbelief into mirrors
Is this how far we have come today?

Now that we are of sunlight
All blue skies now
What are we if not butterflies in the breeze?
Much beloved drifters with an innocent smile.

Neil Parsons

STREET CHILDREN

She stands forlorn and barefoot,
her cry a stab in the dark,
deep through the hearts of the unblinking.
'Gimmee monee,'
she whines
through crusted teeth on starlit nights,
as she clutches at your skirt
with a hand of hungry bones.
You see, but barely hear
her lostness.
Her matted hair, scoffs your Salon Perfect highlights,
your very pearly whites
are mocked by her lacking.
You yearn to reach out and touch,
but dare not,
because she is beyond
the realms
your small mind can tolerate.
A quick fumble through a purse heavy with change
and a few coins dropped
to a plaintive, 'Thank you Ma'am,'
are the closest to salvation you'll come, this night.

Johanna Castro

DO YOU EVER?

Do you ever wonder how you would feel if you were set free -
free from all lies and all the deceits

Do you ever think how you would react to know, if you were rid of
the anger and pain,
the pain that made you want to stay,
that made you hold onto the hope of 'one day it may just change'

Do you ever sometimes picture you fully walking away,
and if you did it yesterday - where would you be today?

Do you ever?

Do you ever believe you can value a new you,
learn about you,
hold onto you,
even trying loving you?

You see I need to ask this, as I'm sitting here looking in at what
you're going through,
the pain is just breath-taking and it hurts me to know you're accepting
and retaking the rubbish that's right underneath you . . .

Do you ever?

Do you ever see yourself conquering this feeling
by just letting go and stop re-repeating?

Do you ever thank the Lord up above for taking you out a situation
you were once in,
and then realising you're still in the same ole, same ole rut
you dug up yourself, so deep within.

Do you ever?

Well do you?

Veronica Bennett

THE WATCHER

It's cold today, quite bitter, but warm and snug inside.
I sit curled up, near the window seat,
My blanket hugs my legs and feet,
And silently I watch . . .
Watch the tiny children, watch the tiny birds,
Watch a horse and cart go by and count the snowflakes in the sky.
And, oh what joy it brings, to appreciate these things.
Snowballs flying to and fro, bring back those memories,
Of youth and childhood often shared,
Times of laughter, those who cared.
Of passions and desires,
But now my mind it tires.
To see them play so joyfully begins a foolish fantasy.
I dream of running through the snow, holding hands, our hearts' aglow,
Of chasing snowflakes through the air,
And watch them settle in your hair.
I long to skate upon the pond, with tiny hands entwined in mine,
And feel the life return in me, once more for all eternity.
Outside the darkness gathers.
The snowflakes fall so fast.
The children leave, homeward bound.
The birds have gone, there is no sound.
And now I am alone and nothing's changed for me.
I watch the lonesome snowman, my only company.
I watch him through my window, whilst in my wheelchair,
And just as lonely he looks back, with pity in his stare.

Julie Eddy

ANGELS

A myriad of lights
all around,
like a veil of stars
they sweep the ground.

In the sky
they are a radiant sight,
like sparkling jewels
in the night.

They swarm about me
like fireflies,
shining brightly
before my eyes.

Moving close
I feel their heat,
like a kindling fire
beneath my feet.

At their touch
my whole body glows,
and to their heavenly realm
my spirit flows.

Mark D Holt

CAT AND MOUSE

Cat and mouse go out to play
Oh what a lovely day
Cat convinces mouse he's friend not foe
'Be careful mouse,' squawks a crafty crow,
Who was 'in the know'.

Cat pats mouse with a delicate paw
Concealing the tip of a sharpened claw
'What game is your choice?'
Purred cat in a velvety voice.
'I like hide and seek,'
Mouse replied with a squeak.

Mouse take care
Venture only if you dare,
To seek cat hidden in the grass
Watching you, bold as brass

Joyful mouse finds cat
Mouse is the winner
Cat licks his chops
Not winner - but dinner

Wily cat
No wonder you are so fat!

Christine Clayton-Owen

POETRY BY NUMBERS

It is clear to me
that poetry and numbers do not mix.
I acknowledge the sonnet form
with its patronising nod
to the ordered world of mathematics
but find it constricting.
Poetry like love
should eschew the container
and salmon like
attack the odds
it should challenge every rock and waterfall
as it strives to reach
the water gods.

Dai Blatchford

OUR OWN PERSONAL ANGEL

(Respectfully dedicated to my very dear grandmother, the late
Mrs Marjorie Crossley, who is still, and indeed always will be
'Our own personal angel')

Our own personal angel was always there when we needed her.
Our dearly departed Marjorie would genuinely have both the time
And the patience to hear us.
With her truly lovely words and her very kindly deeds,
She constantly shone as an amazingly powerful beacon
In a dark world filled with ceaseless despair.
No sincerely delightful soul such as her should ever have
Endured the most painfully horrible afflictions imaginable.
Now our still greatly cherished loved one is peacefully thriving
Within our heavenly Father's real paradise,
Such is where there is only permanently bountiful contentment
                                                    to be found.
Dearest, we certainly wish you well,
As we will indeed confidently see you again,
Never more to be parted from one another.
For you must surely be our own personal angel.

Michael Denholme Hortus Stalker

THE TRAVELLERS

Have you ever noticed when there's nothing on your feet
All the many lines and wrinkles that from toes to ankle meet,
Then they travel round the underneath to meet the other side
And it seems the same on either foot if slim or very wide?
Then sitting looking at your toes they're looking back at you
As if they're saying they're happier bare not stuffed in some old shoe.
So it seems a shame to wrap them up to never see the light
'Cause they need the sun to kiss them or they'll just stay deathly white.
For the wrinkles on your feet are just the same as on your face
And you can't hide those for they all know each wrinkle has its place.

Paddy Jupp

TODAY, NATURE LOVED ME

Her foliage fangs
of yin yang
provided the gift
of a smooth grass grip
(I held to avoid the fall of hell)
her yielding earth around hips.
She caressed lessons of losing to live
staring with cycloptic blinding
attention
she casts the mandatory shadows
of love's fermentation
as I inhaled her particles
of past articles
her wind agitates
past fates
and she exhumes my
buried communes
but they don't gather
smoking meteor showers
or fling in disdain
acidic ice silver rain
or erupt
or disrupt.
They have enriched my ditch
provided roots of experience
so I emerge delirious
there is no justice
there was no crime
just the cycle of time.

Linsey Summers

WHAT WOULD IT TAKE?

What would it take? I asked myself,
To be successful like my friend?

'Take what you want,' he said to me,
'The world's your oyster, don't you know?'

What would it take, I asked myself,
To be successful like my friend?

My education, I surmised,
Would be the key that I would need.

'Take what you want,' he said to me,
'I've no degree, but lots of charm.'

What would it take, I asked myself,
To be successful like my friend?

A logical and searching mind,
Would be the thing to get ahead.

'Take what you want,' he said to me,
'If your face fits, you'll do alright.'

What would it take, I asked myself,
To be successful like my friend?

'Take what you want,' he said to me,
'Take what you want, but don't take mine.'

Mary McManus

THE DEVIL AND I GO WALKING

Tell me again how love conquers death,
For I know naught but the pain of existence.
Tell how colour beautifies all things,
For I am blinded by the horror of life.

Show me how a drop of water revives a flower long dead,
For my nourishment is but the flesh of man.
Show me how a man may sacrifice his life for another,
For I know only the wicked side.

If I be of your world show me what you see,
For if then I see no such thing
Then the devil is me.

John Pullen

WHISPERS FROM THE DARK

I run, run, run
Panting but silent
Run, run, run
No, they won't catch me,
They whisper one step behind me,
We'll catch you, we'll catch you,
I can feel them
Weaving their breath into my mouth
Gagging and hushing me
In their webs like vicious spiders.
I hear my mind screaming
But no one hears.
I thrash my arms
And run, run, run.
A cracking branch above my head
Makes me blanch
They won't stop me,
I'll run through their fluid arms
And trip them in the bushes
We'll catch you, we'll catch you.
The whispers suck my brain
But I run, run, run.
I have only one aim,
Reach my house,
Open the door,
I run, run, run, run
And blast them with the bright light
Into the night.

Airiam

GHOSTS

Whispers in the night,
The fear I cannot fight.
Footsteps in the dark
Echo in my heart.

The whispers of a scream
Reflect in my dreams.
The hammering on the door
Makes me shiver the more.

The things that I have seen
They're not always in my dreams.
The spirits race around my head.
My heartbeat threatens to stop me . . . dead!

I can feel the cold
And upon my soul I'll hold.
The spirits - they near,
I cannot control my fear.

The blanket - above my head.
I fear I might soon be dead.
But I must take a peek.
Is it me they really seek?

I look up from beneath the cover
And there is nothing to discover.
The room is bare
Except for me, a bed and an empty chair.

Angela G Pearson

THE WOLF

Hear the wolf, he's knocking at your door,
Do you answer, or do you ignore?
Death is near, and round the corner,
But there's no need, for a lonely mourner.
    It's time to rejoice, and celebrate,
For the garden is open, and you're at the gate.
You've ended this life, to start another,
and one that will have, a sister and brother.
    You've gone to rest, in the garden of peace,
So your heart, and worries cease.
In this life, so many questions why?
Without a thought, you've learned to fly.
    The wolf is waiting, for you to follow,
Please don't fill, your heart with sorrow.
The sea of souls, you hear it calling,
One more step, you will be falling.
    You miss your child, each and every day,
You cannot find the place she's lay.
Go now my child, go now and play,
Go play until, your waking day.
    No more pain, no more rain,
This life was driving, you so insane.

Dan Del'Ouest

HALFWAY TO . . .

Which way? Which way? Which . . ?
Footsore in midlife's twilight,
On a bone-bleached moor -

We've worn out youth to get here:
Following a primrose path
That petered out, way back!

The old God's failed us.
So we made newer, better, higher,
Impregnable deities -

That crumbled in the warm winds.
And left us stranded, seasick, unable
To decipher our own scribblings.

We've abandoned the vehicle,
Ignored the signpost. Left the motorway.
Looking for policies, societies, moralities,

Philosophies, technologies, therapies . . .
Somewhere, there's a footpath
Not shown on the map.

Jill Truman

HEADLESS HECTOR THE NOISY SPECTRE

Hallowe'en! And I fear mad Sir Hector
Has been walking the West Wing again,
For at night I hear moans and the creaking of bones
And the ominous rattling of chain.

He's turned up each year since they topped him.
At the spot where his victims were slaughtered.
It must be quite daunting to contemplate haunting
When once you've been hung, drawn and quartered.

But they must have re-fitted his entrails
For the task for which Hector was fated.
And one has to admit he's surprisingly fit,
For a man from his head separated.

The vicar prescribed exorcism,
As the way noisy ghosts could be grounded.
But the cleansing routine just made Hector more keen,
To judge by the way that he sounded.

I've tried guard dogs and man traps and mothballs,
Made up balms for his aches and his pains,
I've renewed rusty locks and I've knitted him socks,
Bought some Castrol for oiling his chains.

Kept awake by his shrill lamentations,
I sought out the finest throat tonic,
And I hired a man from La Scala, Milan,
To make Hector's voice more harmonic.

But nothing, it seems, could deter him
From these spectral cacophonous jaunts.
So, I've just called to say that I'm going away
Till I hear it's close season for haunts.

Norman Ford

STURGEON

Demonstrating a luminous illustration
against ceramics,
white, with green waters of Yi Chang
damnations, rounded round
the race track
clockwise with wisdom,
defined by humans
as, luxury on a tip of tastebuds,
debased, perhaps, like lies
enfused inside disgust;
sturgeon rise flow to six feet or more
by refraction,
distorted eyes, drawn toward conclusion.

Graham J Fairbrass

SOME TSUNAMI . . .

Today is calm.

The end of the ocean licks the land,
salt fingers idle townward,
chortling shingle laughs into
new born pools shattering
a thousand iridescent suns
into faceted frenzy.
Seaweed ambassadors inspect
the beach on spume horses

But today is calm

Yesterday, some tsunami or
savage Gods incandescent rage
turned you tiger and
towered you townward maiming
terrified beach huts
murdering screaming deckchairs
hurtling delinquent shingle at
dark hollow-eyed cafes

But today . . . today is calm.

Archie Wilson

BATTLE ABBEY

Perched on the top of Senlac Hill
The famous ancient Norman shrine,
Scene of our brave King Harold's stand,
To face a fearsome battle line.

From Stamford Bridge to meet the foe
Who dared to cross our Sussex coast.
Swift to engage the enemy
And stem the strong invading host.

Our English archers stood their ground
Their long bows claiming many dead,
A cunning ruse betrayed their cause
When Norman ranks appeared to have fled,

In face of guile - the swift pursuit,
The Saxons swarming down the bank,
Were caught in ambush, when they turned
And loosed their arrows, then point-blank.

Discharging arrows by the score,
Pointing them upwards to the sky
To decimate the Saxon force,
Wounding King Harold in the eye.

Which caused the Saxons need to pause
And rally round their stricken King,
Mortally wounded, on the ground,
Abandon force and everything.

And so the Normans won the day,
Chasing our archers up the slope
And clearing all before them, then
England's defenders gave up hope.

So William built the Abbey there
As tribute to his victory.
The Norman Conquest thus begun
Embroidered in our history.

Leonard T Coleman

BIRTH OF THE ANGEL

God spoke: 'Let there be life, unwanted, struggling life in you
Protected by the law,' in nineteen sixty-two.
Miss Young consented, and in time brought forth:
'One Stephen Peter, martyr by my act, or big man with the flaw.
The world will see. Perhaps he'll wear both coats.
I cannot keep him. Head and face present unwanted memory.
Take him and love him well. I've given all I can.

His name is Michael now. 'Who is like God?' it means.
The nurses ask: 'Does Michael do abortions?'
Yes, too well. He fits the bits together.
'Take it away, it's nothing now,
Nothing we want to see.'

Mark Richard

DAYS OF YESTERDAYS

On a day that we die, a child will be born.
We close our eyes and think of the things
That come to us now. As I drop to my knees
And cry, will roses die and fade away. And
Will Romeo's heart bleed forever more?
And lonesome cowboys sing songs of young
Guns gone by. Of heroes from dust to bone how
Once did ride through canyons now gone by.
And did the eagle soar high above us then, with
An eye he did cast over shadows now gone by.
And in a darkened room would a child cry out,
As things would creak with shadows about. Wide
Eyed he would look about, no doubt he'll sleep tonight.
And will heavens above cry out tonight of thunder and
Lightning, and rain will fall upon us tonight, to drown our
Sorrows away. And the mists of the morning lie over like
Satin silk. As the sun will rise and cloud will break of
Distant thunder. Are those the days of yesterdays that soon
Have passed us by.

Craig Alan Hornby

HOOVES 'N' HOUNDS

Bells had been rung,
Carols had been sung,
Gifts had been given,
As I passed beneath the Litchgate,
Walkin' turkey 'n puddin off my belly,
             my lovely belly,

When at once the pink jacketed boy sat in pompous splendour,
Crop in hand, crop in hand,
Drinking from his stirrup cup, stirrup cup,

Against a blue, blue day,
For crisp was the day,
When the hunt did meet, that St Steven's Day.

Where roofs tumbled in on Hooves 'n Hounds
Sniffin' 'n' kickin' at cobbled stones,
Makin' ready for the chase,
            The chase,

Good wishes were exchanged,
When surrounding the names of our fallen,
As blood was in the air,
The ground would surely give up its spirit,
              its spirit,

With a single shot, a mortal shot,
Polluting waters, teaming with life,
Leaving the joke to be explained,
For the wishbone had been broken,
            broken,

Between town and country men,
Between town and country men.

Andrew Fry

CLOUDSWIMMERS

Iodine cloud bulks
blotched into dumb negative
on a litmus paper sky;
shuttling landmass
as white as truth. Islands and plates,
sky perimeter proof,
lovingly plumed
but as blind as butterscotch -
swimming long like winter, and rolling.

When she parts her hair under the water,
it feels like ghosts or clouds;
she holds her arms out
and balances on tiptoes.
Holding her breath,
gravity bereft,
and overcome by caramel synthesis
she swims into
the grease stain-on-paper sky.

Robert Hammond

SUBMISSIONS INVITED
SOMETHING FOR EVERYONE

POETRY NOW 2002 - Any subject,
any style, any time.

WOMENSWORDS 2002 - Strictly women,
have your say the female way!

STRONGWORDS 2002 - Warning!
Age restriction, must be between 16-24,
opinionated and have strong views.
(Not for the faint-hearted)

All poems no longer than 30 lines.
Always welcome! No fee!
Cash Prizes to be won!

Mark your envelope (eg *Poetry Now) 2002*
Send to:
Forward Press Ltd
Remus House, Coltsfoot Drive,
Peterborough, PE2 9JX

**OVER £10,000 POETRY PRIZES
TO BE WON!**

Judging will take place in October 2002